DREAM SHOES
COLORING
BOOK

DREAM SHOES
COLORING
BOOK

SIRIUS

SIRIUS

This edition published in 2024 by Sirius Publishing, a division of
Arcturus Publishing Limited,
26/27 Bickels Yard, 151–153 Bermondsey Street,
London SE1 3HA

ISBN: 978-1-3988-4349-3
CH012199NT

Printed in China

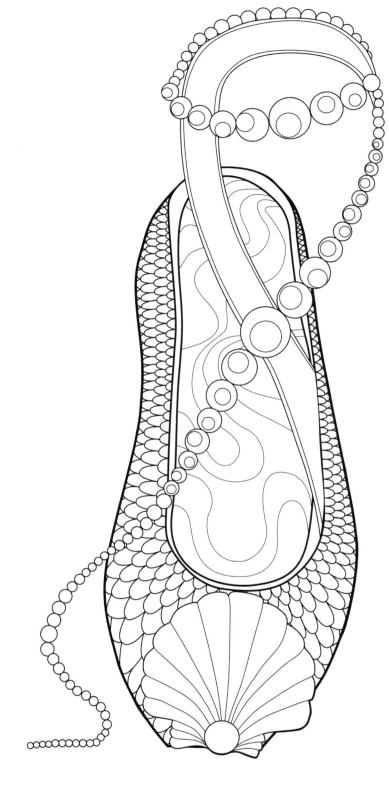

Introduction

Throughout history, shoes have been both a truly functional piece of clothing, offering protection to the foot, and a form of expression. They could indicate a person's status and occupation, signaling that they were ready to hoe a field or dance a ballet. Or they might be so impractical and impossible to walk in that the wearer had to be carried everywhere in a sedan chair!

In more recent times they have been the easiest way to subscribe to fashion trends, to make an old outfit look new, and the wearer stand or walk differently. This collection of "dream shoes" gives the opportunity to create a whole closet full of amazing footwear, from pumps to platforms, and sturdy boots to stilettos. All are a delight to color, so make your selection and start to design your own fantasy shoes.

I would hate
for someone to
look at my shoes
and say, 'Oh my
God! They look
so comfortable!'

Christian Louboutin

*Give a girl
the right shoes
and she can
conquer the
world.*

Marilyn Monroe

I ♥ SHOES

Good shoes take you good places.

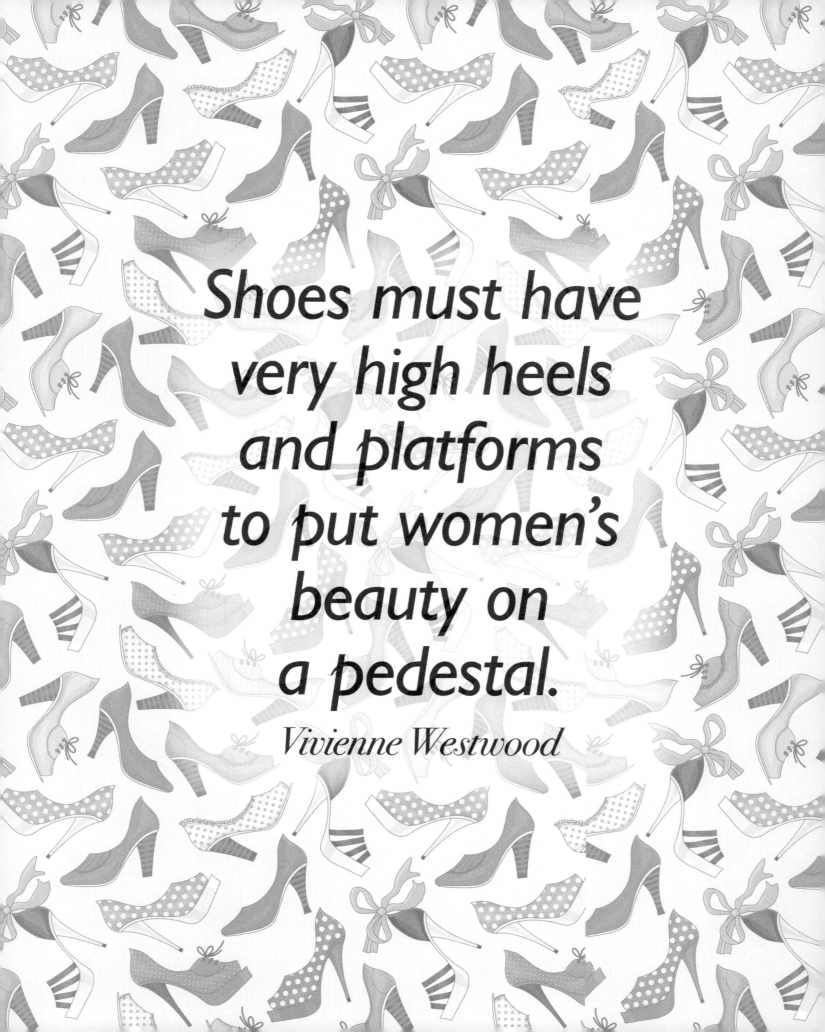

Shoes must have
very high heels
and platforms
to put women's
beauty on
a pedestal.

Vivienne Westwood

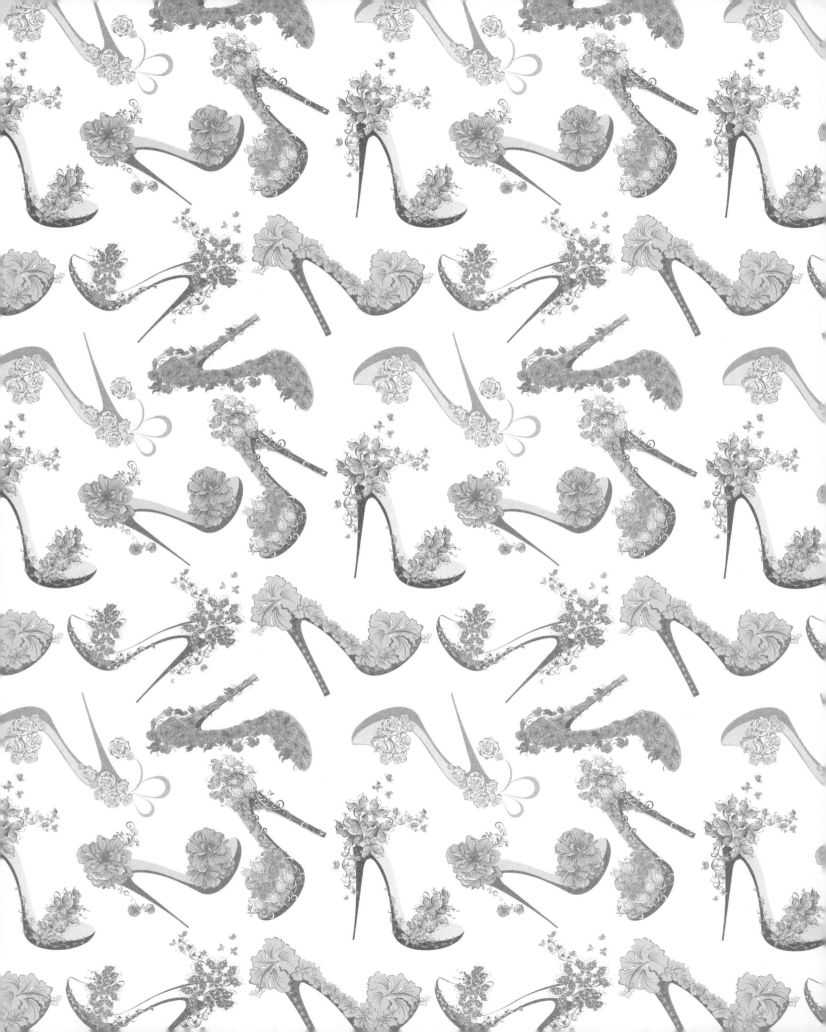

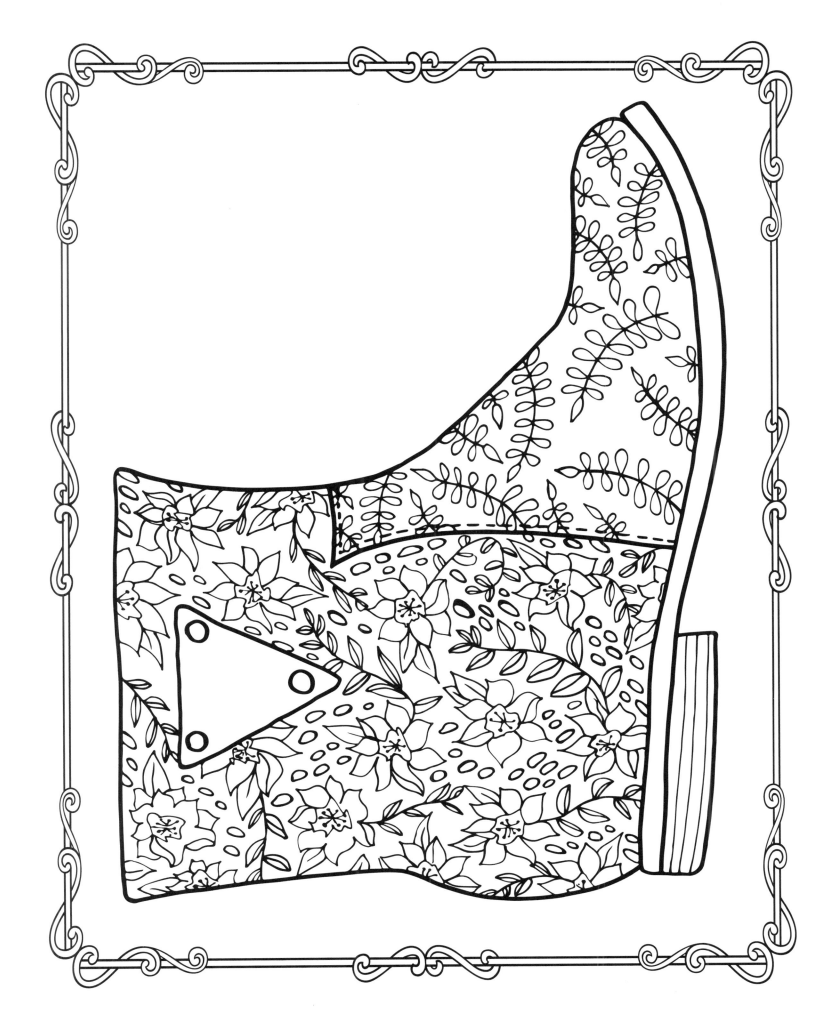

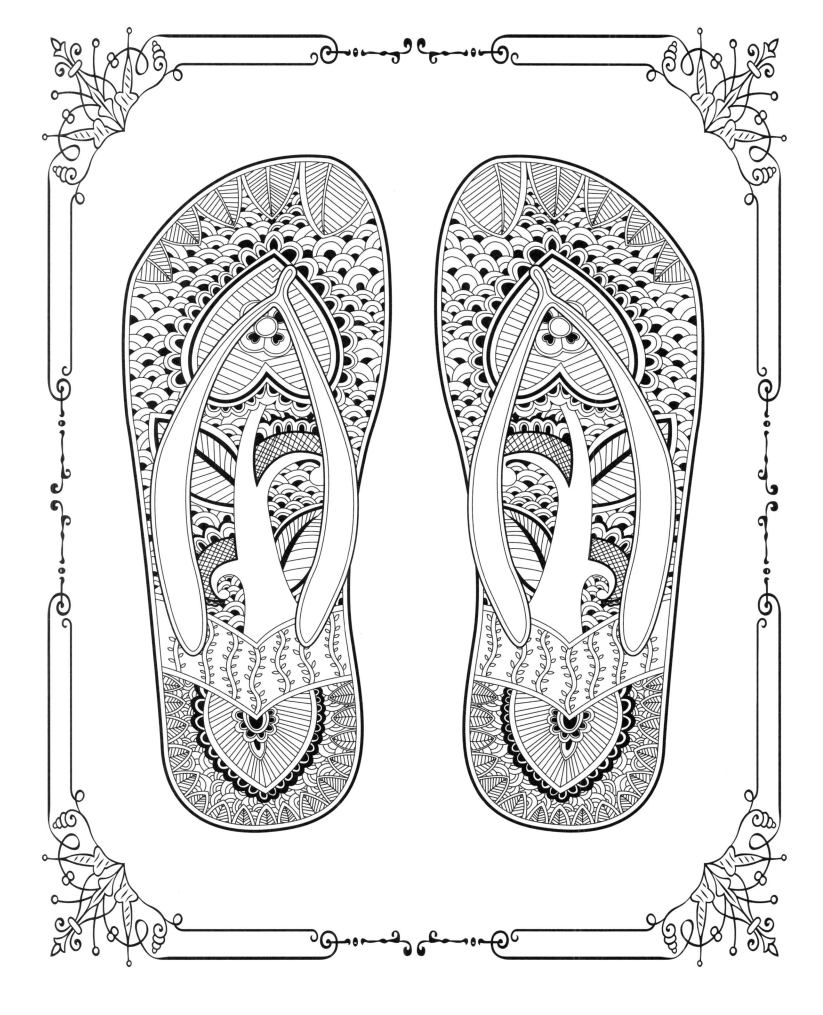

*Cinderella
is proof that
a new pair
of shoes
can change
your life.*

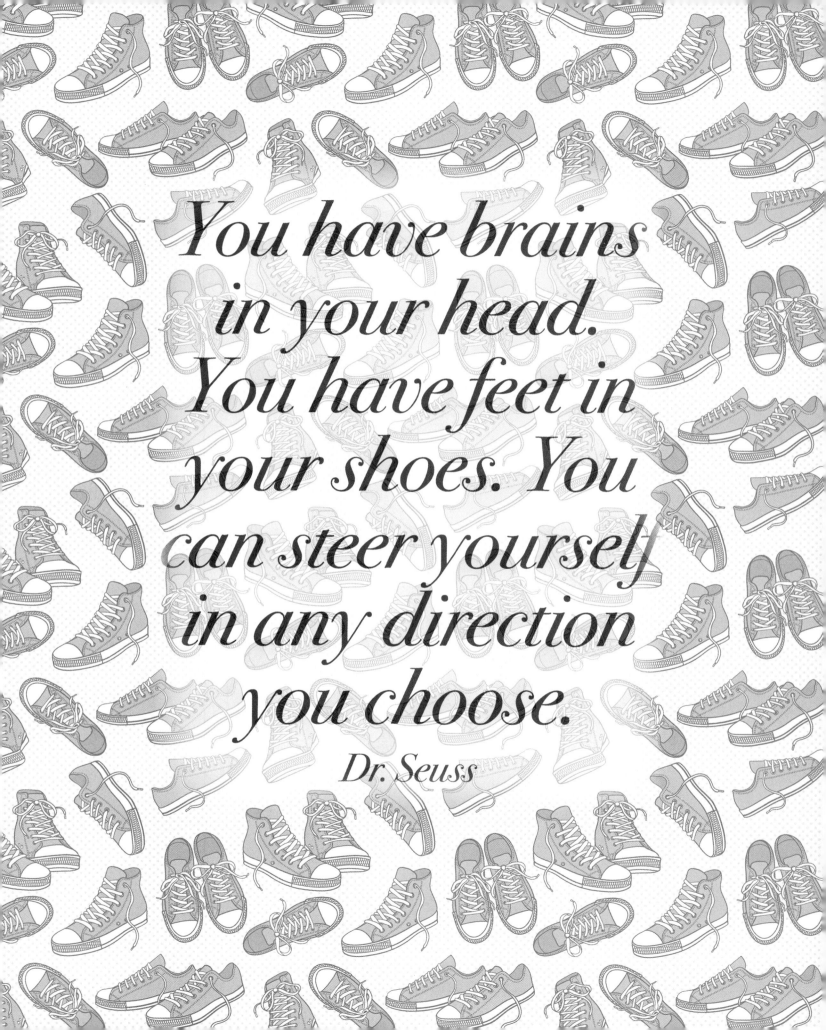

You have brains in your head. You have feet in your shoes. You can steer yourself in any direction you choose.

Dr. Seuss

Fun footwear is a great way to jazz it up and make your ensemble more interesting.

Christian Siriano

With no man in sight, I decided to rescue my ankles from a life of boredom. By purchasing too many pairs of Jimmy Choo shoes.'

Carrie Bradshaw

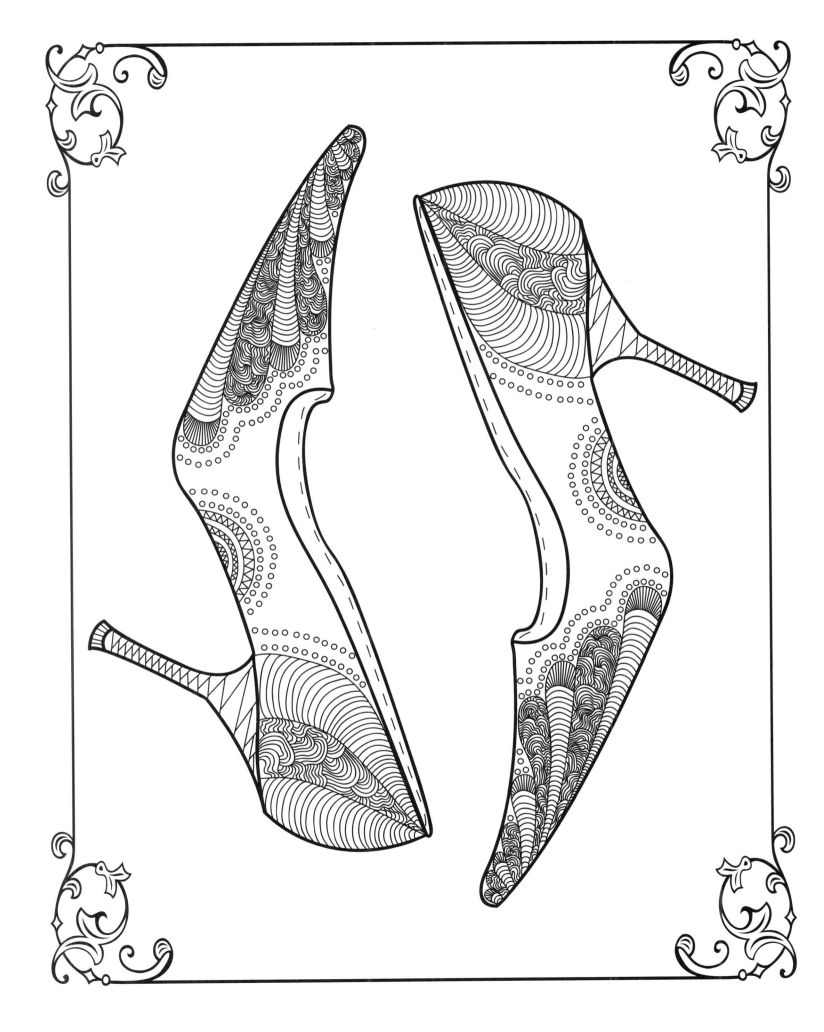

*I can't
concentrate
in flats.*
Victoria Beckham

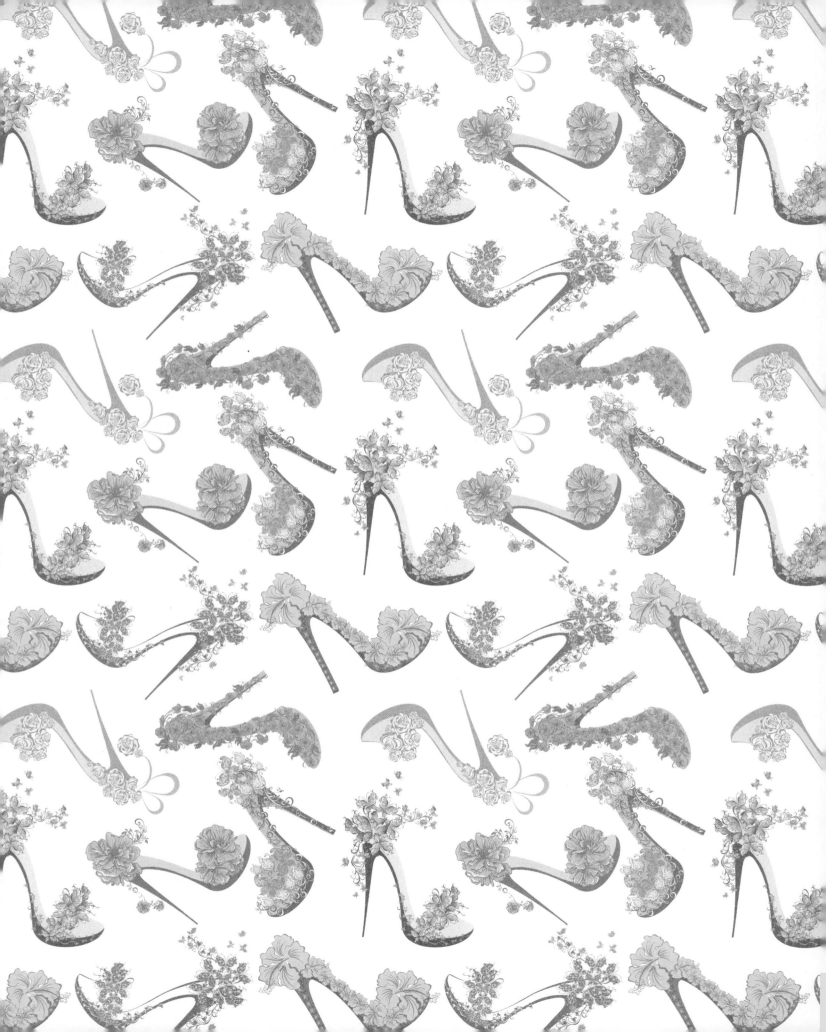

So many
shoes and
only
two feet.

How can you live the high life if you do not wear the high heels.

Sonia Rykiel

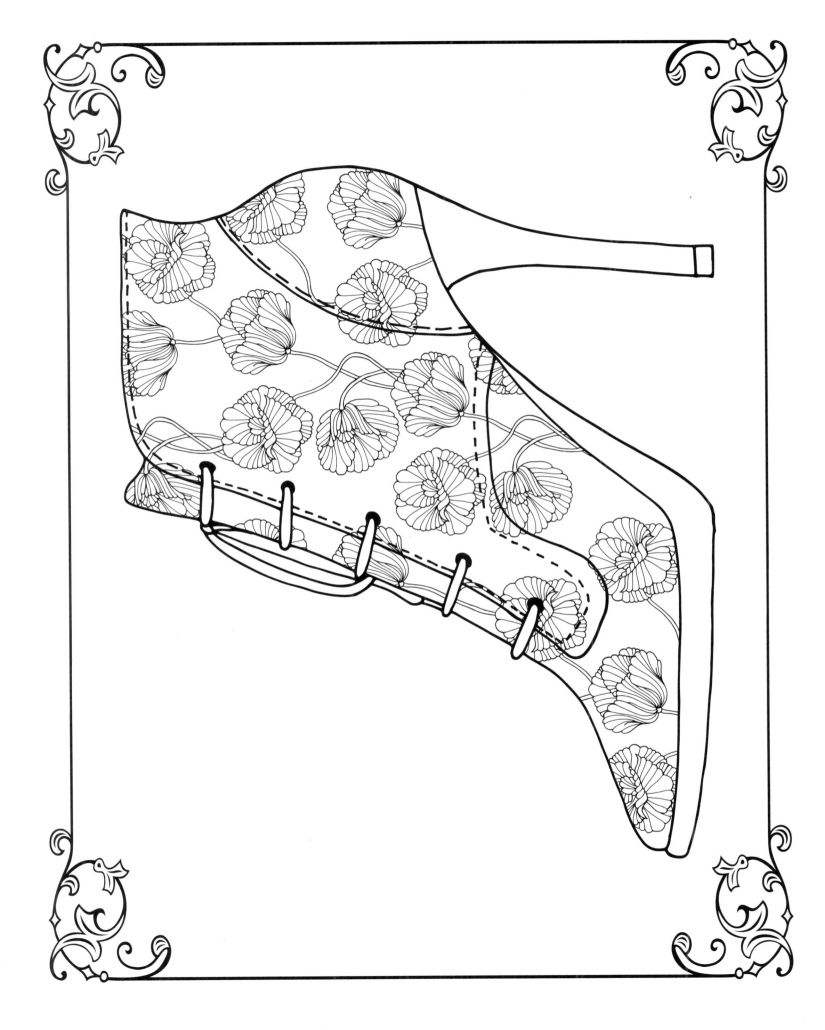

Shoes are the quickest way for women to achieve instant metamorphosis.

Manolo Blahnik

I ♥ SHOES

Life's too short.
Buy the shoes,
drink the wine,
order the dessert.

Keep your head, heels and standards high.

Lola Stark

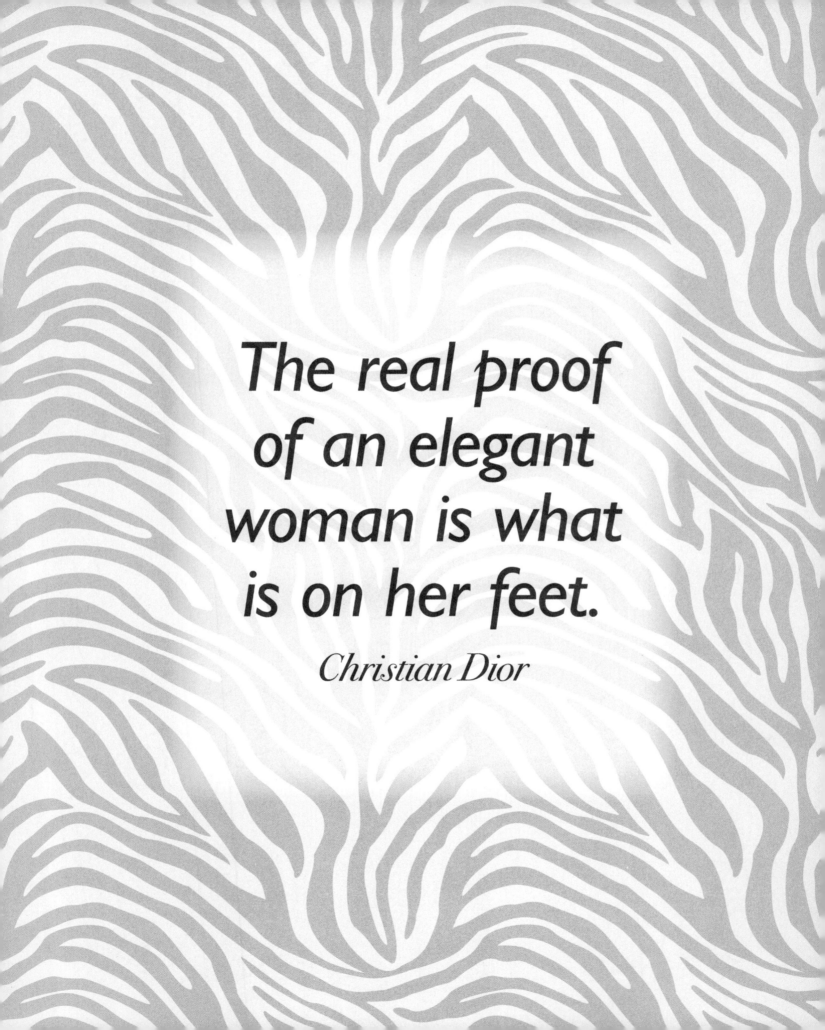

The real proof
of an elegant
woman is what
is on her feet.

Christian Dior

Shoes are like dessert, there's always room for more.

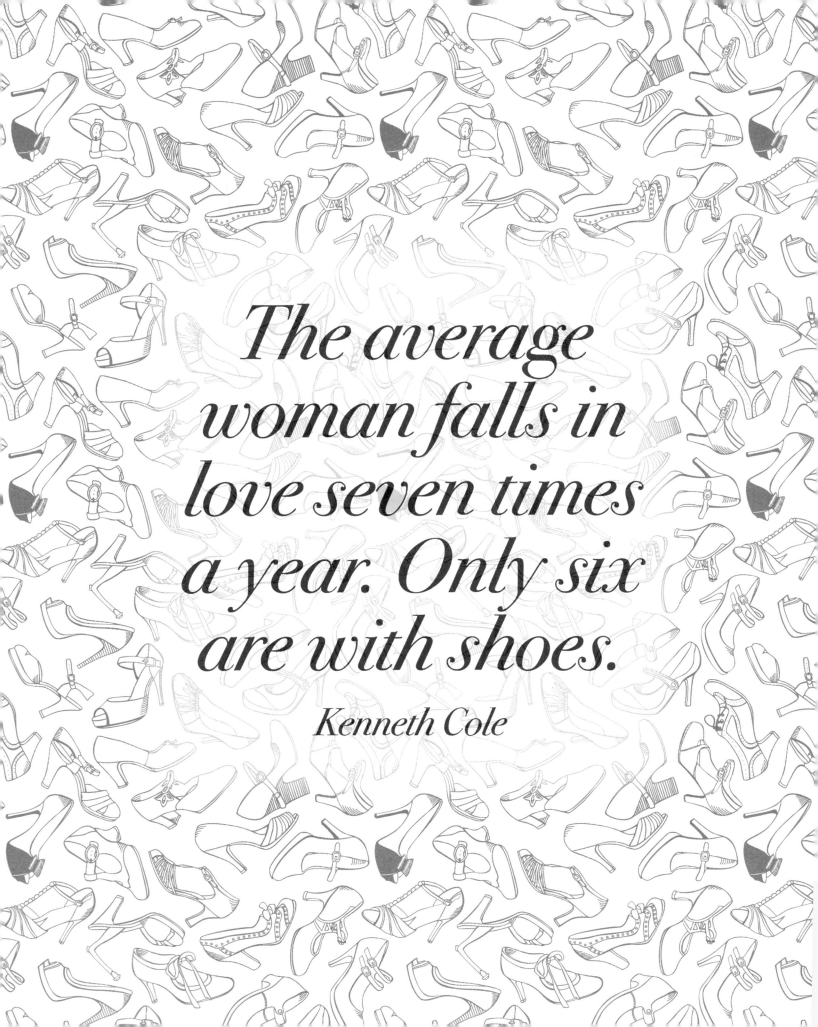

The average woman falls in love seven times a year. Only six are with shoes.

Kenneth Cole

When your feet start to hurt, place yourself in someone else's shoes.

Demi Lovato

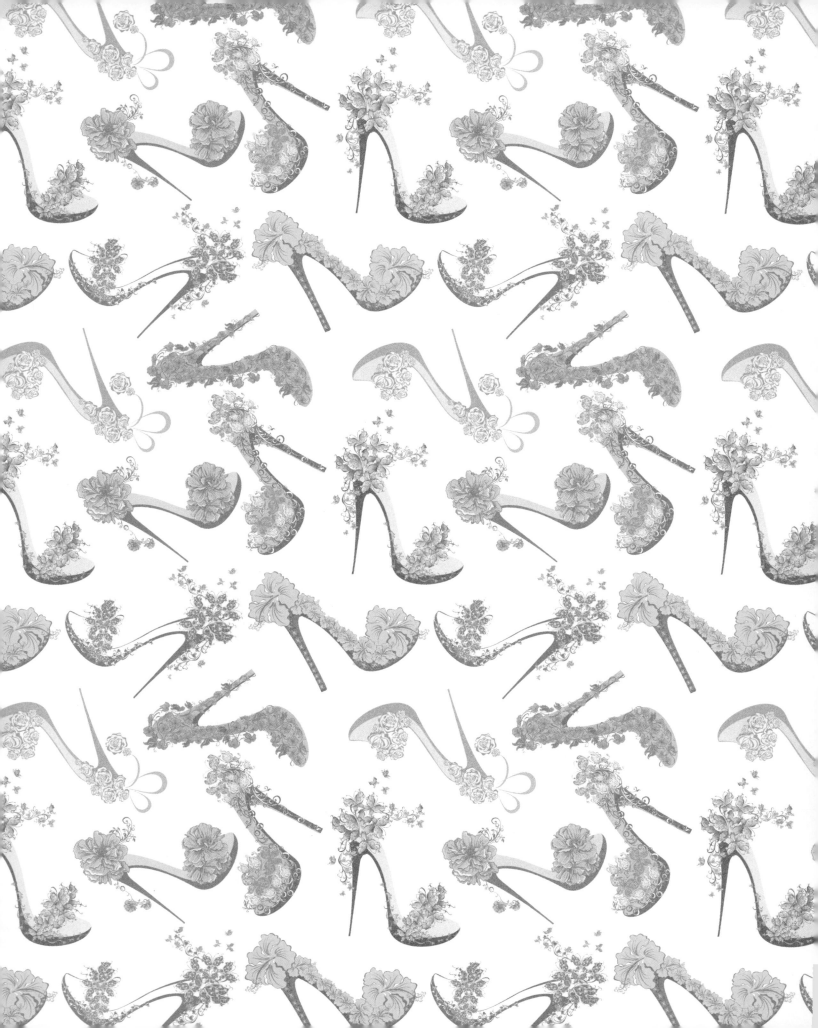

I will literally be the old woman who lived in her shoes.

Carrie Bradshaw

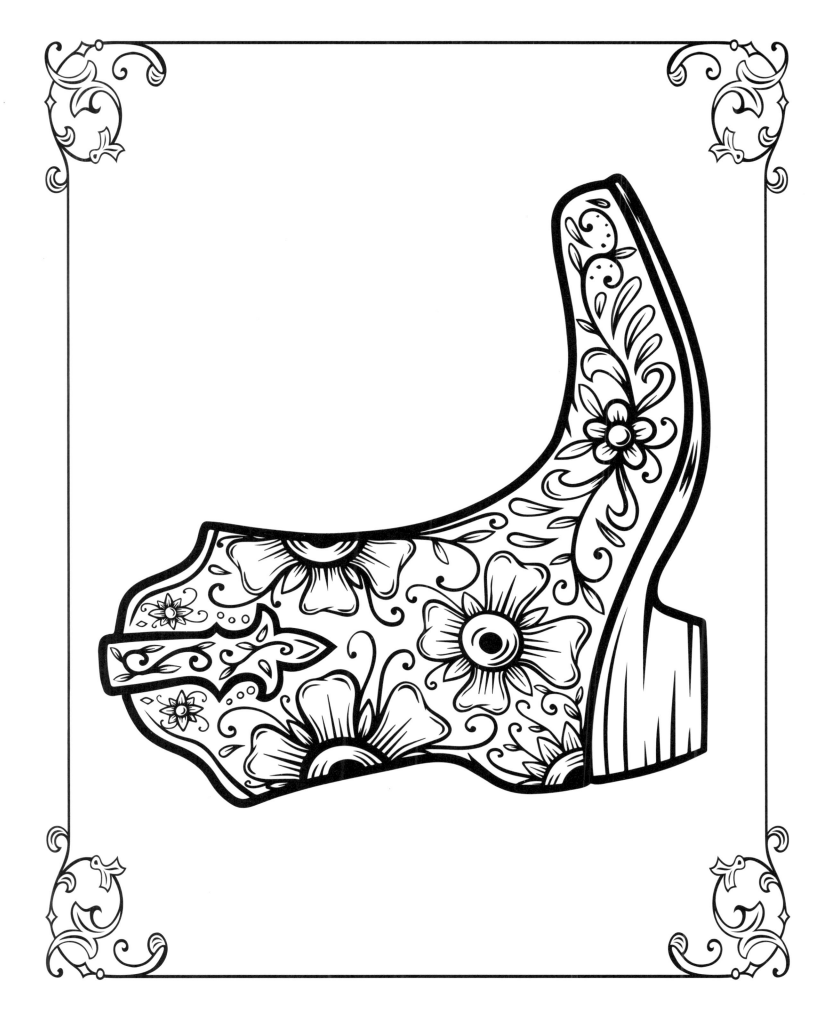

I make shoe contact before eye contact.

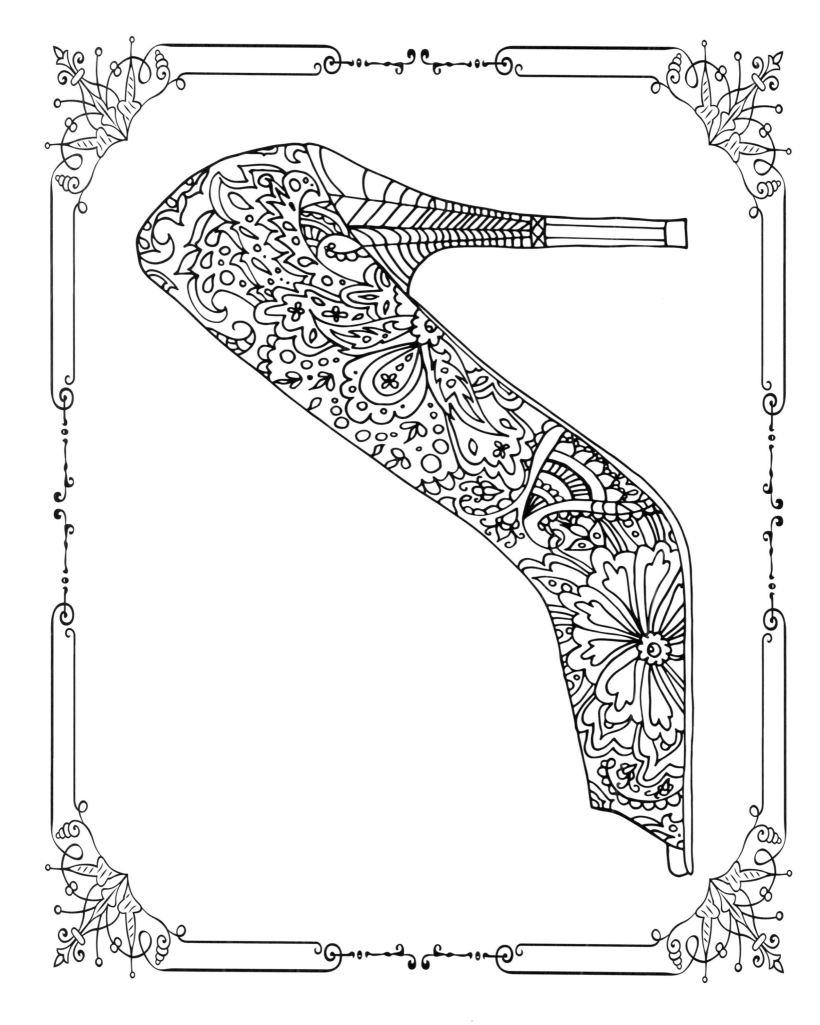

'One shoe
can change
your life.

Cinderella

GREYSCALE

BIN TRAVELER FORM

Cut By _Sandra Soyer_ Qty _31_ Date _12/11/2024_

Scanned By _____ Qty _____ Date _____

Scanned Batch IDs

_____ _____ _____

Notes / Exception

_____

_____

_____

_____

_____